THE REALITY OF THE
HISTORICAL PAST

The Aquinas Lecture, 1984

THE REALITY OF THE HISTORICAL PAST

Under the auspices of the
Wisconsin-Alpha Chapter of Phi Sigma Tau

by

PAUL RICOEUR

MARQUETTE UNIVERSITY PRESS
MILWAUKEE
1984

Library of Congress Catalogue Card Number: 84-060012

© Copyright 1984
Marquette University

ISBN 0-87462-152-6

Prefatory

The Wisconsin-Alpha Chapter of Phi Sigma Tau, the National Honor Society for Philosophy at Marquette University, each year invites a scholar to deliver a lecture in honor of St. Thomas Aquinas.

The 1984 Aquinas Lecture *The Reality of the Historical Past* was delivered in the Todd Wehr Chemistry Building on Sunday, February 26, 1984, by Paul Ricoeur, Professor of Philosophy at the University of Paris.

Professor Ricoeur was born in Valence, France in 1913. He attended the University of Rennes and then the University of Paris where he was awarded the *agrégation de philosophie* in 1935 and *docteur ès lettres* in 1950. He taught at the University of Strassbourg (1948-57) and after that at the University of Paris. He has been visiting professor at Yale University, the University of Montreal, the University of Louvain, and the University of Chicago. He holds honorary degrees from the University of Basel, the University of Montreal, the University of Chicago, the University of Nijmegen, Ohio State University, De Paul University, the University of Zurich, and Boston College.

His main philosophical works are: *Gabriel Marcel et Karl Jaspers. Philosophie du mystère et philosophie du paradoxe* (1948); *Philosophie de la volonté* I. *Le voluntaire et l'involuntaire* (1950) [English: *Freedom and Nature. The Voluntary and Involuntary*]; *Philosophie de la volonté* II. *Finitude et culpabilité* 1. *L'homme faillible* (1960) [English: *Fallible Man*]; *Philosophie de la volonté* II. *Finitude et culpabilité* 2. *La symbolique du mal* (1960) [English: *The Symbolism of Evil*]; *De l'interprétation, Essai sur Freud* (1965) [English: *Freud and Philosophy: An Essay on Interpretation*]; *Le conflit des interprétations: Essais d'herméneutique* (1967) [English: *The Conflict of Interpretations: Essays in Hermeneutics*]; *The Religious Significance of Atheism* (1969); *La Métaphore vive* (1975) [English: *The Rule of Metaphor*]; *Interpretation Theory: Discourse and the Surplus of Meaning* (1976).

Professor Ricoeur has served for many years as editor of *Revue de Métaphysique et Morale.* Of his many published articles a number have been translated and published in *Political and Social Essays* (1974).

To Professor Ricoeur's distinguished list of publications Phi Sigma Tau is pleased to add: *The Reality of the Historical Past.*

The Reality of the Historical Past

What does the term "real" signify when it is applied to the historical past? What do we mean when we say that something really happened?

This is the most troublesome question that historiography puts to historical thinking. And yet, if it is difficult to find a reply, the question itself is inevitable: it makes the difference between history and fiction, whose interferences would pose no problem if they did not grow out of a basic dissymetry.

A solid conviction animates the historian here: regardless of the selective nature of collecting, preserving, and consulting documents, and of their relation to the questions put to them by the historian, even including the ideological implications of all these manoeuvres – the recourse to documents marks a dividing line between history and fiction. Unlike the novel, the constructions of the historian are intended to be reconstructions of the past. Through documents and by means of documentary proof, the historian is constrained by *what once was*. He owes a *debt* to the past, a debt of *gratitude* with respect to the dead, which makes him an *insolvent debtor*. This is the conviction that is expressed by the notion of trace. Inasmuch as it is *left* by the *past*, it *stands for* the past, it "represents" the past, not in the sense that the past would appear itself in the mind *(Vorstellung)* but in the sense that the trace takes place of *(Vertretung)* the past, absent from historical discourse. I shall thus venture to speak of *taking-the-place-of* in order to distinguish the relation of *Vertretung* from that of *Vorstellung*. It characterizes the *indirect* reference specific to knowledge through traces and distinguishes from any other the referential mode of the history of the past.[1] This referential mode is inseparable from the work of configuration itself: for it is only by means of the unending rectification of our configurations that we form an idea of the inexhaustible resources of the past.

This problematic concerning taking-the-place-of or representing history in relation to the past is no longer a question posed by the historian but by the philosopher. It concerns the manner of *thinking* of history rather than historical *knowledge*. For the historian, the notion of trace constitutes a sort of *terminus* in the series of referrals that, from archives, lead to the document, and from the document to the trace. However, the historian does not usually linger over the enigma of historical reference, over its essentially indirect character. For the historian, the ontological question implicitly contained in the notion of trace is immediately covered over by the epistemological question of the document, namely, its value as warrant, support, proof in the explanation of the past.[2]

In the pages that follow, an attempt will be made, if not to resolve, at least to articulate the enigma of *representing* or of *taking-the-place-of*: we shall attempt to say what is original in the historical past's position of *vis-à-vis* in relation to the *limiting-concepts* of critical thinking. In Kant their negative function is clearly predominant: the thing-in-itself is purely unknowable and its positing by *thought* is meant to limit the claims of thought through representation or through objects – which is the same thing – to know things as they are and the noumenal ego as it is. With the idea of the past, the undeniably positive features of the limiting-idea come to the forefront: something once took place.

What is no longer, one day was. This pre-
dominance of the positive side of the limiting-
idea is evident in that it is the past *such as*
it was that moves historians to provide historical configurations and that is behind their
endless rectifications, as they touch up the
painting. This is what I wanted to suggest
when I spoke of the historian's *inexhaustible
debt* with respect to the past. The past is thus
a guiding-concept as much as a limiting-
concept.

The question is then to know if the gap that
is opened in this way between the historian's
vis-à-vis and Kantian limiting-concepts does
not express the very originality of the idea
for the past in relation to the *thing-in-itself*,
which carries no temporal mark.

It is this properly temporal specificity of the
vis-à-vis that we are now going to explore.

I propose, more for didactic than for dialectical reasons, to place the idea of historical
past under the incomparable categories that
Plato in the *Sophist* called the "great classes."
For reasons that will become more apparent
as our work of thinking progresses, I have
chosen the three great classes of the Same,
the Other, and the Analogue. I do not claim
that the idea of the past is constructed dialec-

tically by the very interconnection of these three great classes, I merely hold that we are talking sense about the past by thinking of it, in turn, under the sign of the Same, then of the sign of the Other, and finally under that of the Analogue.

1. Under the sign of the Same: "Re-enacting" the past in the present.

Under the sign of the Same I place the conception of history as "re-enactment" of the past, following Collingwood.[3] The discussion will show in what way this conception calls for, as its counterpart, that of the past as history's *absent* partner.

In order to avoid any confusion, it is important to indicate at the outset Collingwood's true place in the philosophy of history. *Re-enactment* is not a method of understanding – even less of explanation – which would take its place somewhere between William Dray and Henrik von Wright. The fact that it has served as a warrant for intuitionist variations of understanding and that, as such, it is generally dismissed by most epistemologists has done it a great disservice. From this stems the

major misunderstanding concerning Collingwood's work, which is that of a philosopher
more than that of an epistemologist. From the
outlying regions of epistemology, Collingwood moves into the realm of philosophy,
which he defines in the Introduction to *The
Idea of History* as thought about thought.[4]
Three themes are connected to this second-
order reflection. They concern: a) the *documentary* character of historical thought;
b) the work of *imagination* in the interpretation of documentary data; c) finally, the desire
that the constructions of the imagination *re-
enact* the past. The theme of re-enactment
must be maintained in third place, in order
clearly to indicate that it does not designate
an alternative method but the result aimed
at by documentary interpretation and by the
constructions of the imagination.[5]

The interpretation of documents is so
closely tied to the definition of history that
it suffices to distinguish the history of human
affairs from the study of natural changes,
including that of evolution in biology.[6] More
precisely, the notion of documentary proof,
placed at the forefront of the investigation
refers directly to the problem that concerns
us, that of knowledge through traces. Of

what, exactly, are documents the trace? Essentially, of the "inside" of events, which has to be called *thought*. Not that the "outside" of the event, that is to say the physical changes affecting bodies, is itself inessential. On the contrary, *action* is the union of the inside and the outside of an event. This is why the historian is the one who is obliged "to think himself into the action, to discern the thought of its agent" (213).[7] On the other hand, the term "thought" has to be taken in a broader sense than that of rational thought; it covers the whole field of intentions and motivations, to the extent that a desire can figure in the major premise of a practical syllogism by its character of desirability, which is hypothesized to be expressible. This vast sense given to thought allows us to say that knowing *what* happened is already knowing *why* it happened (214).

This twofold delimitation of the concept of "historical evidence" by means of the notion of the "inside" of the event and that of the "thought" of the historical agent leads directly to that of re-enactment. To introduce oneself through thought into an action in order to discern in it the thought of its agent is precisely to *re-think* in one's own mind what was once thought. This sudden access to re-enactment has, nevertheless, the drawback of giving support to the idea that re-enactment is a type of method: "All history," it is affirmed, "is the re-enactment of past thought in the historian's own mind" (215). On the other hand, a warning is contained in the very definition of re-enactment: re-enacting does not consist in reliving but in rethinking, and rethinking already contains the critical moment that forces us to take the detour by way of the historical imagination. [8]

The document, in fact, raises the question of the relation of historical thought to the past as past. But it can only raise it: the reply lies in the role of *historical imagination* that marks the specificity of history in relation to the observation of a given present, as in perception. [9] The section on "historical imagination" is surprisingly audacious. Confronting the authority of written sources, the historian is his own source, "his own authority" (236). His *autonomy* combines the selective character of the work of thought, the audacity of "historical construction," and the tenacity of the suspicions of the one who, following Bacon's adage, "puts Nature to the question." Nor does Collingwood hesitate to speak of "*a priori* imagination," to signify that the historian is the judge of his sources and not the opposite. The criterion for his judgement is the coherence of his construction.

All intuitivist interpretation, that would situate the concept of re-enactment on a methodological plane, is excluded: this plane is occupied by the imagination.[11]

The notion of re-enactment enters in on the level of historical *thought*, at the point where the historical construction, which is the work of the *a priori* imagination, makes its own truth claim. In this sense, it was necessary to extend the *constructed* character of the historical picture as far as possible in order to sharpen the paradox of re-enactment. Unlike the novelist, the historian has a double task: to construct a coherent picture, one that makes sense, and "to construct a picture of things as they really were and of events as they really happened" (246). The second task is only partially accomplished, if one considers the "rules of method" that distinguish the work of the historian from that of the novelist: localizing all historical narratives in the same space and the same time, being able to relate all historical narratives to a single historical world, making the picture of the past agree with the documents in their known state or as historians discover them. If one were to stop at this, the problem of the past as such would not arise; for to localize events in the same space and in the same time not implying the notion of the present is also to leave aside the notion of the past. This is why, in the paragraph on the historical imagination, Collingwood frankly states that "as Descartes might have said . . . the idea of the past is an 'innate" idea" (247). [12]

The idea of re-enactment is precisely intended to still the scandal caused by this recourse to the innate idea of the past, which upholds the definition of history as "an imaginary picture of the past" (248). But it stills the scandal by abolishing the temporal distance between the past and the present by the very act of *rethinking* what was once thought. This abolishing constitutes the philosophical – hyper-epistemological – signification of re-enactment.

It is first formulated in general, but unequivocal terms in the first paragraph of the *Epilogomena* ("Human Nature and Human History"). Thoughts, it is stated, are in a sense events happening in time, but in another sense, for the person who is concerned with the act of re-thinking, thoughts are not in time at all (217).[13] The fact that this thesis is put forward in the context of a comparison between the ideas of human *nature* and of human *history* is easy to understand. It is in nature that the past is separated from the present: "The past, in a natural process, is a past superseded and dead" (225). In nature, instants die and are replaced by others. On the other hand, the same event, known historically, "survives in the present" (225).

But what does it mean to survive? Nothing, outside of the act of re-enactment. All that is finally meaningful is the current possession of the activity of the past. Might it be objected that it was necessary that the past *survive* by leaving a trace, and that we become *inheritors* of the past in order to be able to re-enact past thoughts? Survival and inheritance are natural processes. Historical knowledge begins with the way in which we enter into possession of them. One could say, paradoxically, that a trace becomes a trace of the past only when its pastness is abolished by the intemporal act of rethinking the event as thought from inside. Re-enactment, understood in this way, resolves the paradox of the trace in terms of *identity*; while the pheno-

menon of the mark, the imprint, and that of
its perpetuation are purely and simply sent
back to the sphere of natural knowledge. The
idealist thesis of the mind's own self-
production, already visible in the concept of
a priori imagination, is simply crowned by the
idea of re-enactment.[14]

This is a radical solution that dispells the
problem instead of resolving it: what do the
notions of process, acquisition, incorporation,
development, and even criticism become if the
event-character of the act of re-enactment is
abolished? How can an act that abolishes its
own difference in relation to the original crea-
tion still be called re-creation? By a rebound
effect, the historicity of the act of taking
possession reintroduces that of acquisition
and poses anew, in an even sharper way, the
question of the *survival of the past in the present*, without which there would by no reason
to speak of re-enacting, rethinking, or re-
creating. The re- prefacing all these expressions itself abolishes the operation that was
intended to abolish it.

Collingwood was not unaware of the diffi-
culties inherent in his identity thesis.

He dismisses a minimalist interpretation,
according to which re-enactment would imply

two acts having the same content (or the same object). A numerical difference between the acts would be compatible with a specific identity. This elegant solution, however, is mistaken in plunging the acts of thinking back into the flow of time, whereas through re-enactment they are freed from the constraints of time. One must, therefore, have the courage to say that there is only one act of thinking, one and the same act, which lasts for a certain lapse of time and which then exists again after a certain time. It is the same activity that is re-enacted in the historian's own mind: this is possible because thought is maintained outside the temporal flow.[15]

The maximalist interpretation runs up against the objection that the historian does not know the whole of the past but only his own thought; and yet history is possible only if the historian knows that he is re-enacting an act that is not his own. Collingwood replies only to that part of the objection concerning the possibility of historical knowledge to take a distance from itself. Yes, thought can think itself as re-enacting a past thought. But is this taking a distance from itself the same thing as creating a distance between oneself and another? Is the sort of otherness that self-distancing implies the same as that which distinguishes someone else's thought from my own? Collingwood's entire enterprise collapses when confronted with the possibility of passing from the thought of the past as *mine* to the thought of the past as *other*. The notion of re-enactment expresses the audacious effort to resolve the otherness of repetition in terms of the identity of reflection.

At the same time, Collingwood's failure indicates the direction to be pursued: his theory of re-enactment decomposes the notion of historical time into two notions, both of which deny it. On one side we find change, where one occurrence replaces another; on the other, the intemporality of the act of thinking: the survival of the past which makes the trace possible, tradition which makes us its heirs, and preservation which allows new possession. These mediations cannot be placed under the "great class" of the Same.

2. Under the sign of the "Other": A negative ontology of the past?

Dialectical reversal: if the past cannot be thought under the great category of the Same, could it be grasped better under that of the Other?

In those historians who remain open to philosophical questioning, we find a number of suggestions which, despite their diversity, point in the direction of what could be called a negative ontology of the past.

Taking the opposite tack from Collingwood, many contemporary historians see in history an admission of otherness, a restitution of temporal distance, even an apology for difference, pushed to the point of temporal exoticism. But very few have ventured to cast in theoretical terms this pre-eminence of the Other in historical *thought*.

The concern with recovering the sense of temporal *distance* stands in opposition to the ideal of re-enactment when the main emphasis is placed, in the idea of historical inquiry, on *taking a distance* with respect to the temptation of or the attempt at "empathy." Problematization then predominates over received traditions, and conceptualization over the simple transcription of lived experience in its own language; history then tends as a whole to *make the past remote* from the present. It can even expressly attempt to produce an effect of strangeness in contrast to the desire to make the unfamiliar familiar again, to use Hayden White's vocabulary.

And why would the effect of strangeness not go so far as to make us feel we are in a foreign, unknown land? The historian has only to become the ethnologist of days gone by. This strategy of putting-at-a-distance is placed in the service of the attempt at spiritual *decentering* practiced by those historians most concerned with repudiating the Western ethnocentrism of traditional history.[16]

Under what category can we think of taking-a-distance in this way?

It is not without importance that we begin with what is most familiar to the authors influenced by the German tradition of *Verstehen*: the understanding of *others* is for this tradition the best analogue of historical understanding. Dilthey was the first to found all the human sciences – including history – on the capacity the mind possesses to transport itself into an alien psychic life, on the basis of signs that "express" – that is, carry to the outside – another's personal experience. Correlatively, the transcendence of the past has as its first model the alien psychic life carried outside by "signitive" conduct. A bridge is thus built from two sides; on the one hand, expression crosses the gap separating the outside and the inside; on the other hand, the transfer in imagination into an alien life spans the gap separating the self and its other. From these two converging externalizations results the first objectification by which a private life and an alien life open up one to the other. Onto this first objectification are grafted the second-order objectifications resulting from the inscription of the expression in lasting signs – first and foremost among these, writing.[17]

The model of other people is certainly a very solid one inasmuch as it not only involves otherness but joins the Same to the Other. But the paradox is that by abolishing the difference between others today and others of yesteryear, it obliterates the problematic of temporal distance and eludes the specific difficulty related to the survival of the past in the present – a difficulty that constitutes the difference between knowledge of other people and knowledge of the past.[18]

Another logical equivalent of the *otherness* of the historical past in relation to the present has been sought in the notion of *difference*, which, in its turn, lends itself to multiple interpretations. We pass from the pair same-other to the pair identity-difference, without noticeable variations of meaning other than contextual. But the notion of *difference* lends itself, in its turn, to a wide range of uses. I shall consider two of these, borrowed from professional historians concerned with fundamental reflection.

One way to make use of the notion of difference in an historical context is to couple it with that of individuality, a notion that the historian necessarily encounters in correlation with that of historical "conceptualization."[19]

It is this use of the term "difference" that Paul Veyne emphasizes in *L'Inventaire des Différences*. In order for the individual to appear as difference, historical conceptualization must itself be conceived of as the search for and the positing of *invariants*, understanding by this term a stable correlation between a small number of variables capable of generating their own modifications. The historical fact would then have to be grasped as a *variant* generated by the individualization of these invariants.[20]

But how can a logical difference constitute a temporal difference? Paul Veyne seems at first to admit this, to the extent that he substitutes for the investigation of the distant, as temporal, that of the event characterized in the least temporal manner possible in terms of its individuality.[21]

In this way the epistemology of the individual can appear to eclipse the ontology of the past. If explaining in terms of invariants is the opposite of recounting, this is indeed because the events have been detemporalized to the point of being neither near to us nor far away from us.[22]

Actually, individualization by the variation of an invariant and individualization by time do not coincide. The former is relative to the scale of specification of the invariants selected. In the logical sense, it is true to say that in history the notion of individuality is only rarely identified with that of an individual in the ultimate sense: marriage in the peasant class under Louis XIV is an individuality relative to the problematic chosen, without there being any question of recounting the life of the peasants considered one by one. Individuation by time is something else: it is what makes the *inventory of differences* not an intemporal classification, but an involvement in narratives.

We return in this way to the enigma of *temporal distance*, an enigma overdetermined by the axiological distancing that has made us strangers to the attitudes of past ages, to the point that the otherness of the past in relation to the present overrides the survival of the past in the present. When curiosity takes over from sympathy, the foreigner becomes foreign. The distance that separates is substituted for the difference that joins together. By the same token, the notion of difference loses its transcendental purity as a "great class" due to its overdetermination. Along with its transcendental purity it also loses its univocity, inasmuch as temporal distance cannot be valued in opposite senses at the same time, depending on whether the ethics of friendship (Marrou) or the poetry of estrangement (Veyne) predominates.

I want to conclude this review of the various figures of otherness with Michel de Certeau's contribution, which seems to me to go farthest in the direction of a negative ontology of the past.[23] This, too, is an apology for difference but in a context of thought that pulls it in almost the opposite direction from the preceding one. This context is that of a "sociology of historiography," in which it is no longer the *object* or the *method* of history that is rendered problematical but the historian himself with regard to his operation.

To do history is to produce something. The question then arises concerning the social place of the historical operation.[24]

Now this place, according to de Certeau, is the unsaid *par excellence* of historiography; in its scientific claim, history indeed believes it is – or claims to be – produced from no particular position, from nowhere. This argument, we note, holds just as much for the critical school as for the positivist school. Where, in fact, does the tribunal of historical judgement reside?

This is the context of questions in which a new interpretation of the event as difference comes to light. How? Once the false claim of the historian to produce history in what approximates a state of socio-cultural weightlessness is unmasked, the suspicion dawns that any history that claims to be scientific is vitiated by a desire for mastery, which sets the historian up as the arbiter of meaning. This desire for mastery constitutes the ideology implicit in history.[25]

By what path does this variety of ideology critique lead to a theory of the event as difference? If it is true that a dream of mastery haunts sciencific historiography, the construction of models and the search for invariants –

and by implication the conception of difference as the individualized variant of an
invariant – also stem from the same ideology
critique. Then arises the question of the status
of a history that would be less ideological. This
would be a history not limited to constructing
models but which would indicate the differences in *deviation (écart)* in relation to these
models. A new version of differences arises
here, resulting from its identification with
that of *deviation*, itself coming out of struc-
tural linguistics and semiology (from Ferdi-
nand de Saussure to Roland Barthes) and
extended by certain contempory philosophers
(from Gilles Deleuze to Jacques Derrida).
However, in de Certeau, difference understood as deviation remains firmly anchored
in contemporary epistemology of history to
the extent that it is the very progress of
model-formation that allows the observation
of deviations: deviations, like Veyne's variants, are "relative to models" (25). But,
whereas differences conceived of as variants
are homogeneous with invariants, deviation-
differences are heterogeneous with respect to
them. We begin with consistency; "difference
is played out at the limits" (27).[26]

Does this version of the notion of difference

considered as deviation offer a better approximation to the event as having-been? Yes, up to a certain point. What de Certeau calls working at the limit puts the event itself in the position of deviation in relation to historical discourse. It is in this sense that deviation-difference contributes to a negative ontology of the past. For a philosophy of history faithful to the idea of deviation-difference, the past is what is missing, a "pertinent absence."

Why then do we not stop with this way of characterizing the past event? For two reasons. First, the deviation is no less relative to an effort of systematization than is the modification of an invariant. Deviations, of course, are excluded from the model, while modifications are included along the periphery of the model. But the notion of deviation remains just as intemporal as that of modification, to the extent that a deviation remains relative to the alleged model. Besides, it is not obvious that the deviation-difference is any more apt than the variant-difference to signify the *having been* that is characteristic of the past. Reality in the past remains an enigma to which the notion of deviation-difference, the fruit of working at the limit, offers simply a sort of negative image, one stripped, moreover, of its specifically temporal aspect.

Of course, a critique of the totalizing views of history, joined to an exorcism of the substantial past and, what is more, to the renouncement of the idea of *representation* in the sense of a mental reduplication of presence, constitute so many cleaning up operations to be performed over and over again. To preside over them, the notion of deviation-difference is a welcome guide. But these are only preliminary manoeuvres. In the final analysis, the notion of difference does not do justice to what seems to be positive in the persistence of the past in the present. This is why, paradoxically, the enigma of temporal distance seems even more opaque at the end of this stripping away. For how could a difference, which is always relative to an abstract system and itself is as detemporalized as possible, *take the place of* what, today absent and dead, was once real and living?

3. Under the sign of the "Analogue": a tropological approach?

The two groups of approaches examined above are not useless to us, despite their unilateral character.

One way of "saving" their respective contributions to the question of history's ultimate referent is to join their efforts together under the sign of the "great class" which itself associates the Same and the Other. The Similar is this great category. Or better, the Analogue which is a resemblance between relations rather than between simple terms.

It is not just the dialectical, nor the merely didactical quality of the series: Same, Other, Analogue that has goaded me on to search a solution to our problem in the direction we are now going to explore. What first caught my attention were the veiled anticipations of this way of categorizing the relation of taking-the-place-of or of representing in the preceding analyses, where we repeatedly encountered expressions of the form: *such as* (such as it was). When one wants to indicate the difference between fiction and history, one unavoidably invokes the idea of a certain correspondence between the narrative and what really happened. At the same time, we are well aware that this re-construction is a different construction than the course of events reported. This is why many authors reject the term "representation" which seems to them to be tainted by the myth of a term-by-term reduplication of reality in the image we have of it. But the problem of correspondence to the past is not thereby eliminated by the change of vocabulary. If history is a construction, the historian instinctively would like this construction to be a reconstruction. It would even appear that this intention to reconstruct by constructing is part of the workload of the good historian. Whether this undertaking is placed under the sign of friendship or under that of curiosity, the historian is moved by the vow to do justice to the past. The relation of historians to the past is first of all that of an unpaid debt in which they represent us all, we the readers of their works. This idea of debt, which may seem strange at first, appears to me to emerge out of an expression common to the painter and to the historian: both seek to "render" a landscape, a course of events. Under the term "render" can be recognized the intention of "rendering its due to what is and to what was."

I have also been guided by a second motive: we are not as unarmed in our efforts to articulate the sense of the term "Analogue" as were the Ancients. Plato does not include it in his list of great classes, although he is familiar with the problem of the "mingling " of the Same and the Other, as is marvelously illustrated by the transcendental combinatory of the *Timaeus*. We have available to us a *rhetorical* theory, and in this rhetoric, a theory of *tropes* in which the similar is mobilized by the strategy of discourse under the figure of *metaphor*. It is this recourse to the theory of tropes, in which metaphor occupies an eminent place, that has made me attentive to Hayden White's effort to elucidate what he calls the "representative" dimension of history through the theory of tropes.

A final reason for advancing boldly in this direction: the tropological treatment of the relation of taking-the-place-of or of representing that holds between the narrative and the past gives me the opportunity to build a bridge between my theory of narrative and my theory of metaphor, as I suggested in the

Foreword to *Time and Narrative,* I. If, as I have tried to show in *The Rule of Metaphor,* metaphor has a referential import, and especially if it makes an ontological claim – if it claims to say *what* things are *like* – forcing us to make a metaphorical use of the verb "to be" itself in the form of "being-as," corresponding to "seeing-as," then the investigation we are going to place under the sign of the Analogue may very well give new luster to rhetoric itself. It then becomes legitimate to ask if it is not in this tropology that the dialectic of the Same and the Other is continued, and if we should not join together at this point the dialectic of the "great classes" and the rhetoric of the "major tropes."

All of these reasons taken together are summed up in the hope that our own concept of the *refiguration* of time by narrative – the core of *Mimèsis* III – will be enriched by an inquiry into the role of figures in the constitution of the relation, taking-the-place-of or representing.

It is at this stage in my reflection that I encounter Hayden White's effort in *Metahistory* and in *Tropics of Discourse,*[27] to complete a theory of emplotment by means of a theory of "tropes" (metaphor, metonymy,

synecdoche, irony). This recourse to tropology
is imposed by the singular structure of historical discourse, in contrast to simple fiction.
This discourse, in fact, appears to call for a
double allegiance: on the one hand, to the constraints related to the privileged *type* of plot,
and on the other, to the past itself through
the documentary information accessible at a
given moment. The historian's work then consists in making the narrative structure a
"model," an "icon" of the past, capable of
"representing" it.[28]

How does the theory of tropes reply to
the second challenge? Reply: ". . . before a
given domain can be interpreted, it must first
be construed as a ground inhabited by dis-
cernible figures" (30). "In order to figure
'what really happened' in the past . . . the
historian must first *pre*figure as a possible
object of knowledge the whole set of events
reported in the documents" *(ibid.)*.[29] The
function of this poetic operation is to trace
out possible itineraries in the "historical field"
and in this way to give an initial contour to
the possible objects of knowledge. The intention is certainly oriented toward what
really happened in the past, but the paradox
is that one can designate what it is that pre-

cedes all narrative only by *prefiguring* it.

The advantage of the four basic tropes of classical rhetoric is that they offer a variety of figures of discourse for this work of pre-figuration and thus preserve the wealth of sense belonging to the historical object, both by the equivocity peculiar to each trope and by the multiplicity of the available figures. [30]

Actually, of the four tropes considered – metaphor, metonymy, synecdoche, and irony – it is the first that has an expressly *representative* function. But White seems to mean that the other tropes, though distinct, are but variants of metaphor, [31] and serve as correctives to the naiveté of metaphor, which tends to hold as adequate the asserted resemblance (my love, a rose). It is not the first time in the rhetorical tradition that metaphor is taken by turns as the generic term and as a species on the level of the tropes. In this way, metonymy, by equating the part and the whole, would tend to make the historical factor the mere manifestation of another factor. Synecdoche, by connecting the extrinsic relation of two orders of phenomena to an intrinsic relation among shared qualities, is held to figure an integration rather than a reduction. Irony is taken to be responsible for introducing a negative note in this work of prefiguration – something like a "second thought." In contrast to metaphor, which inaugurates and in another sense holds the tropological domain together, White calls irony "metatropological," inasmuch as it provokes the awareness of the possible misuse of figurative language and continually recalls the problematical nature of language as a whole. None of these attempts at structuring constitutes a logical constraint and the figurative operation can stop at the first stage, that of metaphorical characterization. But only the complete route from the most naive apprehension (metaphor) to the most reflective (irony) authorizes us to speak of a tropological structure of consciousness.[32] As a whole, the theory of tropes, by its deliberately linguistical character, can be integrated into the table listing the modalities of historical imagination, without thereby being integrated into its properly explanatory modes. As such, it constitutes the deep structure of the historical imagination.[33]

The benefit expected from this tropological chart of consciousness, concerning the *representative* ambition of history, is immense: rhetoric governs the description of the historical field, as logic governs an explanatory argument: "For it is by figuration that the historian virtually *constitutes* the subject of the discourse."[34] In this sense, identifying the type of plot is the domain of logic, but the intention of the series of events that history, as the system of signs, attempts to describe is the province of tropology. Tropological prefiguration proves to be more specific, to the extent that explanation by emplotment is held to be more generic.[35]

We must therefore not confuse the *iconic* value of representation of the past with a model, in the sense of a scale model, like a geographical map, for there is no original given with which to compare the model. It is precisely the strangeness of the original, as the documents make it appear, that gives rise to the effort of history to prefigure the style proper to it.[36] This is why there is no metaphorical relation between a narrative and a course of events: the reader is directed toward a sort of figure that likens the events reported to a narrative form with which our culture has made us familiar.

I should now like to say a few words about where I situate myself with respect to the subtle and often obscure analyses of Hayden

White. I do not hesitate to say that, to me, they constitute a decisive contribution to the exploration of the third dialectical moment of the idea of taking-the-place-of or representing by which I am attempting to express the relation of the historical narrative to the real past. By giving the support of *tropological* resources to the matching up of a given plot with a given course of events, these analyses provide precious credibility to our suggestion that the relation to the reality of the past must move in succession by way of the framework of the Same, the Other, and the Analogue. Tropological analysis is the sought after explicitation of the category of the Analogue. It says only one thing: things must have happened *as* it is stated in the narrative considered. Thanks to the tropological frame of reference, the *being-as* of the past event is brought to language.

Having said this, I readily grant that, isolated from the context of the other two great categories – the Same and the Other – and in particular, released from the constraint that the *vis-à-vis*, the *Gegenüber*, in which the *having-been* of the past event consists, the recourse to the theory of tropes runs the risk of erasing the dividing line between *fiction* and *history*.[37]

By placing the accent almost exclusively on the rhetorical *process,* we are in danger of concealing the intentionality that *crosses through* the "tropics of discourse in the direction of past events." If one did not restore this primacy of the referential intention, one could not say, as White himself does, that the contest between configurations is at the same time "a contest between contending poetic figurations of what the past *might* consist of" (*The Writing of History,* p. 60). I like the formula: "We can only know the actual by contrasting it with or likening it to the imaginable" *(ibid.).* If this formula is to maintain its full force, the concern with "drawing historiography nearer to its origins in literary sensibility" (*ibid.,* p. 61) must not lead us to give more value to the verbal power invested in our redescriptions than to the *incitements* to redescription that come from the past itself. In other words, a certain tropological arbitrariness[38] must not make us forget the kind of constraint that the past exerted on historical discourse through known documents, by demanding an endless *rectification* on its part. The relation between history and fiction is certainly more complex than we can ever say. Of course, we must combat the prejudice that the historian's language could be made entirely transparent, so that the facts would speak for themselves; as if it were enough to get rid of the *ornaments of prose* in order to do away with the *figures of poetry*. But we would be unable to combat this first prejudice if we did not at the same time combat the second, according to which the literature of imagination, because it constantly makes use of fiction, can have no hold on reality. These two prejudices must be fought together.[39]

This is the role that can be assigned to the "great class" of the Analogue in the pursuit of what once was. The aporia of the trace as "standing for" the past finds in *seeing-as* a partial resolution. This *as* was already utilized in Ranke's expression, which has unceasingly goaded us on: the facts *such as* they *really* occurred. In the analogical interpretation of the relation of taking-the-place-of or representing, the accent has shifted from "really" to "such as." Better: *really* has meaning only in terms of *such as.* It is the equivalent of *being as* to which *seeing as* responds and corresponds.

Summing up the whole itinerary of the present study, I would say that the recourse to *analogy* acquires its full sense only against the backdrop of the dialectic of Same and Other: the past is indeed what is to be *re-enacted* in the mode of the identical. But it is so only to the extent that it is also what is *absent* from all of our constructions. The analogue, precisely, holds within it the force of re-enactment and of distancing, to the extent that being as is both being and not being.

It remains that this exploration of the relation of *taking-the-place-of* or of *representing* cannot help but be incomplete – incomplete because it is abstract. As we have learned from phenomenology, and in particular from that of Heidegger, the past, cut off from the dialectic between future, past, and present remains an abstraction. This is why the present study constitutes no more than an attempt to think more clearly what remains *enigmatic* in the pastness of the past as such. By placing it successively under each of the "great classes" of the Same, the Other, and the Analogue, we have at least preserved the mysterious character of the debt which makes the master of plots into a servant of the memory of men of the past.

NOTES

1. I am borrowing from Karl Heussi, *Die Krisis des
    Historismus,* the distinction between *Vertretung* and
    Vorstellung. It replies to the "crisis of historicism"
    inasmuch as the latter, according to the author,
    characterizes not only a period of historiography
    reacting against positivism, but historiography itself
    as such, when it attempts to make its tacit ontological
    presuppositions agree with its explicit epistemological
    developments. The crisis is all the more severe as
    these ontological presuppositions continue to be for-
    mulated within a framework closely related to
    Kantian criticism (the subjective and the objective,
    the absolute and the relative, the normative and what
    becomes, transcendence and immanence), whereas
    the epistemological developments tend to undermine
    the problematic of subject and object. Taking up once
    again the old conflict between the subjective and the
    objective, Karl Heussi introduces the notion of *vis-à-
    vis,* an over-and-against, *Gegenüber* with regard to
    historical knowledge from which the constructions of
    history receive both an incitement and a correction.
    Thinking historically is forming a conception that
    strives to aim at this *Gegenüber,* to "correspond" to
    it in an "appropriate" manner *(eine zutreffende
    Entsprechung des im Gegenüber bewesen,* 98). At this
    point intervenes the notion of *Vertretung:* "the ideas
    of history are *Vertretungen* that claim to signify
    (bedeuten) what once was *(was . . . einst war)* in a con-
    siderably more complicated mode and offered to an
    inexhaustible description" (48). Karl Heussi is correct
    in saying that the problem is no longer that of under-
    standing opposed to explanation but instead that of
    historical *thought.* He continues to reason, however,
    in Kantian terms: "It is clear that the *Gegenüber* is
    a simple limiting-concept." (49). This is why the
    Gegenüber takes on both functions belonging to the

Kantain limiting-concept. It excludes the idea of a ready-made past that would already be constructed in the documents; but it also excludes the conception of a Theodor Lessing for whom history alone would give a meaning to the *meaningless (sinnlos)*, to the extent that the *Gegenüber* imposes a direction and a correction to historical research and even takes away the free choice of the historian with respect to his work of selecting and organizing. For if this were not the case, how could the work of one historian correct that of another and claim to be more accurate *(treffen)*? But Heussi, too, has seen the features of the *Gegenüber* that make the notion of *representing* an enigma proper to historical knowledge. For Heussi, influenced by Troeltsch, "the *Gegenüber* (taken as a whole) remains, to speak in metaphorical terms, the immense, eternally mysterious flow of reality which unfolds in time" (49). By its flowing, the past draws the *Gegenüber* to the side of the meaningless ("It is not only our representations that move along; what moves is also any and every content of the history depicted," 51). But the *multivalent structures* of the past bring it back to the side of the meaningful: the past consists in "the plenitude of possible incitements to historical configuration" *(die Fülle der möglichen Anreize zu historischer Gestaltung)* (49).

2. Marc Bloch's example in *Apologie pour l'histoire; Le métier d'historien* is revealing in this regard. He is well familiar with the problematic of the trace, which presents itself to him through that of the document ("what do we mean by documents, if not a 'trace', that is to say the perceptible mark left by a phenomenon itself impossible to grasp" [56]). But the enigmatic relation of the trace is immediately connected up to the notion of *indirect observation* familiar to the empirical sciences, to the extent that the physicist, the geographer, for example, rely upon observations made by others *(ibid.)*. What differs with respect to the other sciences of observation is indeed to be

sought elsewhere than in the *indirect* nature of the
observation: the historian, unlike the physicist, cannot bring about the appearance of the trace. But this
drawback belonging to historical observation is com-
pensated for in two ways: the historian can multiply
the reports of witnesses, and confront them with one
another; Marc Bloch speaks here of the "handling of
testimonies of opposite types" (65). In particular, the
historian can give precedence to "witnesses inspite
of themselves," that is, to documents that were not
intended to inform or to instruct contemporaries and
even less, future historians (62). For a philosophical
investigation concerned with the ontological import
of the notion of trace, the desire to show that knowledge through traces belongs to the field of observation, tends to conceal the enigmatic character of the
notion of the trace of the *past*. Authenticated
testimony functions like a delegated *eye witness*
account: I see through the eyes of someone else. An
illusion of contemporaneousness is thus created which
allows us to place knowledge through traces along the
line of indirect observation. And yet no one has more
magnificently stressed than has Marc Bloch the bond
of history to time, when he defines it as the "science
of men in time" (36).

3. *The Idea of History* is a posthumous work published
   by T.M. Knox in 1946 (Clarendon Press; Oxford
   University Press, 1956), on the basis of lectures given
   at Oxford in 1936, after Collingwood's appointment
   to the chair of metaphysical philosophy, and partially revised by the author up to 1940. The most complete parts of the manuscript have been grouped
   together by the editor in the fifth part, entitled
   Epilegomena, pp. 205-324.

4. "Philosophy is reflective . . . thought about thought"
   (p. 1). It has opposite it "the past, consisting of
   particular events in space and time which are no
   longer happening" (5). Again: "actions of human

beings that have been done in the past" (9). The
question is: what about them makes it possible for
historians to know them? The accent placed on the
past character of events means that the question can
be answered only by people that are qualified in two
ways, as historians having experience of their profession, and as philosophers capable of reflecting on
this experience.

5. In the table of contents adopted by the editor of *The
Idea of History,* the paragraph on "History as Re-
enactment of Past Experience" (282-302) follows that
on "The Historical Imagination" (231-249) – this was
the first in the series of Oxford lectures, and that on
"Historical Evidence," where the concept of human
history is opposed to that of human nature, and where
re-enactment is examined directly, without passing
by way of the reflection on imagination. This order
of presentation is understandable if re-enactment,
without constituting the methodological process
characteristic of history, defines its *telos,* and with this
its place in knowledge. I shall follow the order:
historical evidence, historical imagination, history as
re-enactment of past experience in order to indicate
that the concept of re-enactment is more philosophical
than epistemological.

6. For Collingwood the question is less knowing how
history differs from the sciences of nature than knowing if there can be knowledge of man other than historical. To this question he gives a clearly negative
answer, for the simple reason that the concept of
human history takes the place assigned by Locke and
Hume to that of human nature: "the right way of
investigating mind is by the methods of history" (209).
"History is what the science of human nature pro-
fessed to be" *(ibid.).* "All knowledge of mind is
historical" (219). "The science of human mind resolves
itself into history" (220). It will be noted that Collingwood calls "interpretation of evidence" (9-10) what we

translate here by *"preuve documentaire"* (documentary proof). Here, he says, "evidence is a collective name for things which singly are called documents, and a document is a thing existing here and now, of such a kind that the historian, by thinking about it, can get answers to the questions he asks about past events" (10).

7. The semiological character of the problem is evident, although Collingwood does not use these terms: external changes are not those the historian looks *at* but *those through which* he looks, in order to discern the thought within them (214). This relation between the inside and the outside corresponds to what Dilthey called *Ausdruck* (expression).

8. "All thinking is critical thinking: the thought which re-enacts past thoughts, therefore, criticizes them in re-enacting them" (216). If, indeed, the cause is the inside of the event itself, then only a long work of interpretation permits us to picture ourselves in the situation, to think for ourselves what an agent in the past judged appropriate to do. Rethinking what was once thought cannot help but be an extremely complex operation, if the original thought already was complex in itself.

9. The relation between historical evidence and imagination situates historical inquiry entirely within *the logic of question and answer*. This is presented in *An Autobiography,* Oxford University Press, 1939. Gadamer himself pays Collingwood a vibrant homage in his own attempt to make this logic the equivalent of Plato's dialogical method, after Hegel's failure. Collingwood is a precursor in this respect: "question and evidence, in history, are correlative. Anything is evidence which enables you to answer your own question – the question you are asking now" (281).

10. Collingwood is not afraid to take as his own Kant's description of imagination as "that blind but indispensable faculty," which "does the entire work of

historical construction" (241). We are here at the opposite end of the spectrum from the idea of eye-witness accounts transmitted by authorized sources: "So there are properly speaking no data" (249). The idealism inherent in the thesis of *a priori* imagination is strikingly apparent in the concluding lines of the paragraph devoted to it: "the idea of historical imagination (is to be held) as a self-dependent, self-determining, and self-justifying form of thought" (249). One must then go so far as to practically identify the work of the historian with that of the novelist. "Both novel and history are self-explanatory, self-justifying, the product of an autonomous or self-authorizing activity; and in both cases this activity is the *a priori* imagination" (246).

11. In this respect the comparison between re-enactment and practical inference, proposed by Rex Martin in *Historical Explanation, Re-enactment and Practical Inference,* Cornell University Pres, 1977, constitutes the most fecund attempt to connect Collingwood up with the philosophy of history practiced by A. Danto, W. Walsh and especially von Wright. Imagination, practical inference, and re-enactment are to be thought together.

12. "Every present has a past of its own, and any imaginative reconstruction of the past aims at reconstructing the past of this present, the present in which the act of imagination is going on, as here and now perceived" (247). Note the sui-referential definition of the present, implied in the referral to the act of imagination as it is perceived here and now.

13. The Roman constitution, or its modification by Augustus, once it is re-thought, is not less an eternal object than Whitehead's triangle: "The peculiarity which makes it historical is not the fact of its happening in time, but the fact of its becoming known to us by our re-thinking the same thought which

created the situation we are investigating, and thus coming to understand that situtation" (218).

14. "Thus the historical process is a process in which man creates for himself this or that kind of human nature by re-creating in his own thought the past to which he is heir" (226). "The historian must re-enact the past in his own mind" (282). Re-enactment thus tends to take the place of testimony, the strength of which lies in maintaining the otherness of both the witness and of what he has been a witness to.

15. *The Idea of History* offers several equivalent expressions: "the subject matter of history," is not the individual act, as it was produced, "it is the act of thought itself, in its survival and revival at different times and in different persons" (303). This implies that self-activity is seen as "a single activity persisting through the diversity of its own acts" (306). And again, "The object must be of such a kind that it can revive itself in the historian's mind; the historian's mind must be such as to offer a home for that revival" (304). "Historical knowledge, then, has for its proper object thought: not things thought about, but the act of thinking itself" (305).

16. This concern with taking a distance is very strong in French historians; François Furet demands, in the beginning of *Penser la Révolution française,* that intellectual curiosity break with the spirit of commemoration or of denouncing. *Un autre Moyen Age,* to use J. Le Goff's title, is the Middle Ages seen as different from our age. For Paul Veyne, in *L'Inventaire des différences,* "the Romans existed in a manner just as exotic and just as ordinary as the Tibetans or the Nambikwara, for example, neither more nor less; so that it becomes impossible to continue to consider them as a sort of value-standard" (8).

17. This model was powerful enough to inspire both Raymond Aron and Henri Marrou: the first part of *Introduction à la philosophie de l'histoire* moves from

self-knowledge to the knowledge of others and from
this to historical knowledge. It is true that, in specific
cases, the argument tends to undermine the apparent
progression suggested by the outline: as self-
coincidence is impossible (59), other people constitute
the genuine mediators between self and itself.
Knowledge of others, in its turn, never reaching the
fusion of consciousnesses, always requires the media-
tion of signs. Finally, historical knowledge, based on
works emanating from consciousnesses, is revealed
to be just as originary as knowledge of others and as
self-knowledge. It results that, for Aron, "the ideal
of resurrection is . . . less inaccessible than foreign
to history" (81). If in Marrou, in *De la connaissance
historique,* the understanding of others remains the
most powerful model of historical knowledge, this is
due to the conjunction of epistemology and of ethics
in historical knowledge. The understanding of others
today and the understanding of men of the past shares
the same, essentially moral, dialectic of same and
other: on the one hand, we know basically what re-
sembles us; on the other hand, the understanding of
another person requires that we perform the *epochè*
of our own preferences in order to understand the
other as other. It is the suspicious attitude of the
positivist historian that prevents us from recogniz-
ing the identity of the tie of friendship that exists
between the self and the other today, and between
the self and the other in the past (118). This tie is more
essential than curiosity, which, in fact, pushes the
other back into the distance.

18. These have often been related to one another in
analytical philosophy due to the similarity between
the paradoxes they give rise to in a philosophy that
holds empirical knowledge, hence present observation, to be the ultimate criterion of verification. Assertions about others and assertions about the past have
in common the fact that they are neither verifiable,
nor capable of refutation in this manner. They also

have in common the ability to be exchanged for one another, up to a certain point, to the extent that what history attempts to reach in the past are basically actions of people like ourselves, and in which, inversely, the knowledge of others, more than self-understanding, contains the same gap between lived experience and retrospection. But these reasons are not enough to make the two problems the same.

19. Cf. Paul Veyne, "la connaissance historique," in *Faire de l'Histoire.* Weber's method of ideal-types had anticipated this movement of thought. But it is French historiography that has most stressed the effect of putting-at-a-distance in relation to historical conceptualization. Conceptualizing is breaking with the point of view, the ignorance, the illusions, and the entire language of people of the past. It is already to make them removed from us in time. Conceptualizing is adopting the regard of mere curiosity, that of the ethnologist – unless it is that of the entomologist . . . .

20. "The invariant," Paul Veyne states, "explains its own historical modifications on the basis of its internal complexity; on the basis of this same complexity, it also explains its own eventual disappearance" (24). In this way, Roman imperialism is one of the two great variants of the invariant of the search for security pursued by a political power; instead of seeking it by means of a balance with other great powers, as in the Greek variant, Roman imperialism searches security by means of the conquest of the entire human horizon "to its very limits, to the sea or to the barbarians, in order finally to be alone in the world when all has been conquered" (17).

21. "The conceptualization of an invariant thus allows us to explain events; by playing on the variants, we can recreate, on the basis of the invariant, the diversity of historical modifications" (19). Put even more forcefully: "The invariant alone individualizes" (19).

22. One must go so far as to say that "historical facts can be individualized without being set into place in a spatio-temporal complex" (48). And again: "History does not study man in time: it studies human materials subsumed under concepts" (50). At this price, history can be defined as "the science of differences, of individualities" (53).

23. "L'opération historique," in *Faire de l'Histoire,* edited by Le Goff and Nora (Paris: Gallimard), 1976, I.

24. "Conceiving of history as an operation would be trying . . . to understand it as the relation between a *place* (a recruitment, a milieu, a profession, etc.) and procedures of analysis (a discipline)" (4).

25. This argument will not surprise readers of Horkheimer and Adorno – the great leaders of the Frankfurt School – who revealed the will for domination at work in the rationalism of the Enlightenment. One finds something similar to this in Habermas's first works, where he denounces the claim of intrumental reason to annex the historico-hermeneutical sciences. Some of Michel de Certeau's statements go much further in the sense of classical Marxism and suggest what, in my opinion, is an altogether too linear and too mechanistic relation between historical production and social organization: "from collecting documents to writing books, the historical practice is entirely relative to the structure of society" (13). "Through and through, history remains configured by the system out of which it develops" (16). On the other hand, what is said about the production of documents and the redistribution of space" (22) that it implies is extremely enlightening.

26. What follows in the text is quite eloquent: "To make use of an old term that no longer corresponds to its new trajectory, one could say that it [research] no longer starts with rare elements (remains of the past) in order to reach a synthesis (present comprehension), but that it starts with a formalization (a present

system) in order to produce remains (indications of limits) and by this to a "past" that is the product (of labor)" (27).

27. *Metahistory. The Historical Imagination in XIXth Century Europe* (Baltimore and London: The Johns Hopkins University Press, 1973), pp. 31-38. *Tropics of Discourse* is the title of a collection of articles published between 1966 and 1978 (Baltimore: The John Hopkins University Press, 1978). I shall be considering mainly the articles written after *Metahistory:* "The Historical Text as Literary Artifact," *Clio* 3, no. 3 (1974); "Historicism, History and the Figurative Imagination," *History and Theory* 14, no. 4 (1975); "The Fictions of Factual Representation," in *The Literature of Fact,* edited by Angus Fletcher (New York: Columbia University Press, 1976). The article published in *Clio* is also included in *The Writing of History,* edited by Canary and Kozecki (University of Wisconsin Press, 1978).

28. "I will consider the historical work as what it most manifestly is – that is to say, a verbal structure in the form of a narrative prose discourse that purports to be a model, or icon, of past structures and processes in the interest of *explaining what they were by representing* them" (*Metahistory,* 2). Further on it is stated: "Historical accounts purport to be verbal models, or icons, of specific segments of the historical process" (30). Similar expressions can be read in articles written after *Metahistory:* the desire to construct "the kind of story that best fitted" the known facts (*The Writing of History,* 48). The historian's subtlety consists "in matching up a specific plot-structure with a set of historical events that he wishes to endow with a meaning of a particular kind" *(ibid.).* With these two image-laden expressions the entire problem of the representation of the past is posed in conjunction with the operation of emplotment.

29. "This preconceptual linguistic protocol will in turn
    be – by virtue of its essentially *prefigurative* nature –
    characterizable in terms of the dominant tropological
    mode in which it is cast" (*Metahistory,* 30). It is termed
    prefigurative, not in our sense (*Mimèsis* I), namely
    as a structure of human praxis preceding the work
    of configuration by the historical narrative or by the
    fictional narrative, but in the sense of a *linguistical*
    operation unfolding on the level of the still indiscri-
    minate mass of documentary data: "By identifying the
    dominant mode (or modes) of discourse, one pene-
    trates to that level of consciousness on which a world
    of experience is *constituted* prior to being analyzed"
    (*Metahistory,* 33).

30. This is why, in opposition to the binarism fashionable
    in linguistics and in structural anthropology, Hayden
    White goes back to the four tropes of Ramus and Vico.
    The 1974 article "Historicism, History and the Figura-
    tive Imagination," offers a well-argued criticism of
    Jakobson's binary analysis. It is not surprising that
    Tropics of Discourse contains several essays that deal
    directly or indirectly with Vico's logical poetics, Vico
    who is shown to be Hayden White's true master, along
    with Kenneth Burke and his *Grammar of Motives* (the
    expression "master-tropes" comes from the latter).

31. I understand in this sense the following statement,
    which at first sight is disconcerting: "Irony, Meto-
    nymy, and Synecdoche are kinds of Metaphor, but
    they differ from one another in the kinds of *reduc-
    tions or integrations* they effect on the literal level
    of their meanings and by the kinds of illuminations
    they aim at on the figurative level. Metaphor is essen-
    tially *re-presentational,* Metonymy is *reductionist,*
    Synecdoche is *integrative,* and Irony is *negational*"
    (*Metahistory,* 34).

32. The problem is taken up again in "Fictions of Factual
    Representation" (*Tropics of Discourse,* 122-144):
    metaphor gives preference to resemblance, meto-

nymy to continuity, hence *dispersion* in mechanical series of relations (it is Burke who is responsible for characterizing dispersion as "reduction"); synecdoche gives preference to the part-whole relation, hence to integration, from which result holistic or organicist interpretations. Irony, suspension, gives preference to contradiction, aporia, by stressing the *inadequacy* of any *characterization.* It is also recalled, as it was in *Metahistory,* that there is a certain affinity between a given trope and a given mode of emplotment: between metaphor and the romanesque, between metonymy and the tragic, etc.

33. The introduction to *Tropics of Discourse:* "Tropology, Discourse and Modes of Human Consciousness" (1-26) ascribes to this "tropical element in all discourse, whether of the realistic or the more imaginative kind," a more ambitious function than that accorded it by *Metahistory:* tropology now covers all the deviations leading from one meaning *toward* another meaning "with full credit to the possibility that things might be expressed otherwise" (2). This field is no longer limited to the prefiguration of the historical field; it extends to any sort or preinterpretation. Tropology bears the colors of rhetoric as it confronts logic, wherever understanding strives to render familiar the unfamiliar or the alien, by paths irreducible to logical proof. Its role is so vast and so fundamental that it can, little by little, become the equivalent of a *cultural critique* of a rhetorical type of all the areas where consciousness, in its cultural *praxis,* enters into a debate with its milieu. Any new system of encoding is, at this deep level, figurative.

34. "Historicism, History and the Imagination," *Tropics of Discourse,* 106.

35. "This conception of the historical discourse permits us to consider the specific *story* as an *image* of the events *about which* the story is told, while the generic story-type serves as a *conceptual model* to which the

events are to be likened in order to permit their en-
codation as elements of a recognizable structure"
(*Tropics of Discourse*, 110). The division between the
rhetoric of tropes and the logic of modes of explanation is substituted for the overly basic distinction
between fact (information) and interpretation (expli-
cation). Conversely, their imbrication in the past
allows us to reply to the paradox posed by Lévi-
Strauss in *The Savage Mind,* based on the fact that
history was held to be torn between a *micro-level*
where events are disolved in aggregates of physico-
chemical reactions and a *macro-level* where history
is lost in the vast cosmologies that rhythm the rise
and decline of civilizations of the past. There is thus
held to be a *rhetorical* solution to the paradox according to which an excess of information ruins understanding and an excess of understanding im-
poverishes information (*Tropics of Discourse,* 102).
Insofar as the work of figuration adjusts *facts* and
explanations to one another, it allows the historian
to stay half-way between the two extremes under-
scored by Lévi-Strauss.

36. As a result of this prefiguration, our historical narratives are no more than "metaphorical statements
which suggest a relation of similitude between such
events and processes and the story types that we con-
ventionally use to endow the events of our lives with
culturally sanctioned meanings" (*Tropics of Discourse,*
88).

37. Hayden White is not unaware of this danger. This is
why he invites us "to understand what is fictive in all
putatively realistic representations of the world and
what is realistic in all manifestly fictive ones" (*The
Writing of History,* 52). In the same sense: . . .we
experience the fictionalization of history as an
explanation for the same reason that we experience
great fiction as an illumination of a world that we
inhabit along with the author. In both we re-cognize

the forms by which consciousness both constitutes and colonizes the world it seeks to inhabit comfortably" (*ibid.*, 61). Having said this, White is not too far away from what we mean by the *interweaving reference* of fiction and of history. But, as he does not really show us what is realistic in all fiction, only the fictive side of the purportedly realistic representation of the world is stressed.

38. "The implication is that historians *constitute* their subjects as possible objects of narrative representation by the very language they use to *describe* them" (*ibid.*, 57).

39. Hayden White readily grants this: novel and history are not simply indistinguishable as verbal artifacts, both of them purport to offer a verbal image of reality. One is not concerned with consistency and the other with correspondence; both, by different paths, aim at consistency *and* at correspondece: "It is in these twin senses that all written discourse is cognitive in its aims and mimetic in its means" (*Tropics of Discourse*, 122). He also states: ". . .history is no less a form of fiction than the novel is a form of historical representation" *(ibid.)*.

Published by the Marquette University Press
Milwaukee, Wisconsin 53233
United States of America

#1 St. Thomas and the Life of Learning (1937)
by John F. McCormick, S.J. (1874-1943)
professor of philosophy, Loyola University.
ISBN 0-87462-101-1

#2 St. Thomas and the Gentiles (1938) by Morti-
mer J. Adler, Ph.D., Director of the Institute of Philosophical Research, San Francisco,
Calif.   ISBN 0-87462-102-X

#3 St. Thomas and the Greeks (1939) by Anton
C. Pegis, Ph.D., professor of philosophy,
Pontifical Institute of Mediaeval Studies,
Toronto.   ISBN 0-87462-103-8

#4 The Nature and Functions of Authority (1940)
by Yves Simon, Ph.D., (1903-1961) professor of philosophy of social thought, University of Chicago.   ISBN 0-87462-104-6

#5 St. Thomas and Analogy (1941) by Gerald B.
Phelan, Ph.D., (1892-1965) professor of phi-
losophy, St. Michael's College, Toronto.
ISBN 0-87462-105-4

#6 St. Thomas and the Problem of Evil (1942) by
Jacques Maritain, Ph.D., professor *emeritus*
of philosophy, Princeton University.
ISBN 0-87462-106-2

#7 Humanism and Theology (1943) by Werner
Jaeger, Ph.D., Litt.D., (1888-1961) Univer-
sity professor, Harvard University.
ISBN 0-87462-107-0

#8 The Nature and Origins of Scientism (1944) by John Wellmuth, Chairman of the Department of Philosophy, Loyola University.
ISBN 0-87462-108-9

#9 Cicero in the Courtroom of St. Thomas Aquinas (1945) by E. K. Rand, Ph.D., Litt D., LL.D. (1871-1945) Pope professor of Latin, *emeritus,* Harvard University.   ISBN 0-87462-109-7

#10 St. Thomas and Epistemology (1946) by Louis-Marie Regis, O.P., Th.L., Ph.D., director of the Albert the Great Institute of Mediaeval Studies, University of Montreal.
ISBN 0-87462-110-0

#11 St. Thomas and the Greek Moralists (1947, Spring) by Vernon J. Bourke, Ph.D., professor of philosophy, St. Louis University, St. Louis, Missouri.   ISBN 0-87462-111-9

#12 History of Philosophy and Philosophical Education (1947, Fall) by Etienne Gilson of the *Académie français,* director of studies and professor of the history of Mediaeval philosophy, Pontifical Institute of Mediaeval Studies, Toronto.   ISBN 0-87462-112-7

#13 The Natural Desire for God (1948) by William R. O'Connor, S.T.L., Ph.D., former professor of dogmatic theology, St. Joseph's Seminary, Dunwoodie, N.Y.   ISBN 0-87462-113-5

#14 St. Thomas and the World State (1949) by Robert M. Hutchins, former Chancellor of the University of Chicago, president, of the Fund for the Republic.   ISBN 0-87462-114-3

#15 Method in Metaphysics (1950) by Robert J. Henle, S.J., Ph.D., academic vice-president, St. Louis University, St. Louis, Missouri.
ISBN 0-87462-115-1

\# 16 Wisdom and Love in St. Thomas Aquinas
(1951) by Etienne Gilson of the *Académie
français*, director of studies and professor
of the history of Mediaeval philosophy, Pontifical Institute of Mediaeval Studies, Toronto.
ISBN 0-87462-116-X

\# 17 The Good in Existential Metaphysics (1952)
by Elizabeth G. Salmon, Ph.D., professor of
philosophy in the graduate school, Fordham
University. ISBN 0-87462-117-8

\# 18 St. Thomas and the Object of Geometry (1953)
by Vincent Edward Smith, Ph.D., director,
Philosophy of Science Institute, St. John's
University. ISBN 0-87462-118-6

\# 19 Realism and Nominalism Revisited (1954) by
Henry Veatch, Ph.D., professor and chair-
man of the department of philosophy, North-
western University. ISBN 0-87462-119-4

\# 20 Imprudence in St. Thomas Aquinas (1955) by
Charles J. O'Neil, Ph.D., professor of phi-
losophy, Villanova University.
ISBN 0-87462-120-8

\# 21 The Truth That Frees (1956) by Gerard Smith,
S.J., Ph.D., professor of philosophy, Marquette University. ISBN 0-87462-121-6

\# 22 St. Thomas and the Future of Metaphysics
(1957) by Joseph Owens, C.Ss.R., Ph.D.,
professor of philosophy, Pontifical Institute
of Mediaeval Studies, Toronto.
ISBN 0-87462-122-4

\# 23 Thomas and the Physics of 1958: A Confron-
tation (1958) by Henry Margenau, Ph.D.,
Eugene Higgins professor of physics and
natural philosophy, Yale University.
ISBN 0-87462-123-2

#24 Metaphysics and Ideology (1959) by Wm. Oliver Martin, Ph.D., professor of philosophy, University of Rhode Island.

ISBN 0-87462-124-0

#25 Language, Truth and Poetry (1960) by Victor M. Hamm, Ph.D., professor of English, Marquette University. ISBN 0-87462-125-9

#26 Metaphysics and Historicity (1961) by Emil L. Fackenheim, Ph.D., professor of philosophy, University of Toronto.

ISBN 0-87462-126-7

#27 The Lure of Wisdom (1962) by James D. Collins, Ph.D., professor of philosophy, St. Louis University. ISBN 0-87462-127-5

#28 Religion and Art (1963) by Paul Weiss, Ph.D. Sterling professor of philosophy, Yale University. ISBN 0-87462-128-3

#29 St. Thomas and Philosophy (1964) by Anton C. Pegis, Ph.D., professor of philosophy, Pontifical Institute of Mediaeval Studies, Toronto. ISBN 0-87462-129-1

#30 The University in Process (1965) by John O. Riedl, Ph.D., dean of faculty, Queensboro Community College. ISBN 0-87462-130-5

#31 The Pragmatic Meaning of God (1966) by Robert O. Johann, associate professor of philosophy, Fordham University.

ISBN 0-87462-131-3

#32 Religion and Empiricism (1967) by John E. Smith, Ph.D., professor of philosophy, Yale University. ISBN 0-87462-132-1

#33 The Subject (1968) by Bernard Lonergan, S.J., S.T.D., professor of dogmatic theory, Regis College, Ontario and Gregorian University, Rome.　　　　　ISBN 0-87462-133-X

#34 Beyond Trinity (1969) by Bernard J. Cooke, S.J., S.T.D., Marquette University.
　　　　　ISBN 0-87462-134-8

#35 Ideas and Concepts (1970) by Julius R. Weinberg, Ph.D., (1908-1971) Vilas Professor of Philosophy, University of Wisconsin.
　　　　　ISBN 0-87462-135-6

#36 Reason and Faith Revisited (1971) by Francis H. Parker, Ph.D., head of the philosophy department, Purdue University, Lafayette, Indiana.　　　　　ISBN 0-87462-136-4

#37 Psyche and Cerebrum (1972) by John N. Findlay, M.A. Oxon, Ph.D., Clark Professor of Moral Philosophy and Metaphysics, Yale University.　　　　　ISBN 0-87462-137-2

#38 The Problem of the Criterion (1973) by Roderick M. Chisholm, Ph.D., Andrew W. Mellon, Professor in the Humanities, Brown University.　　　　　ISBN 0-87462-138-0

#39 Man as Infinite Spirit (1974) by James H. Robb, Ph.D., professor of philosophy, Marquette University.　　　　　ISBN 0-87462-139-9

#40 Aquinas to Whitehead: Seven Centuries of Metaphysics of Religion (1976) by Charles E. Hartshorne, Ph.D., professor of philosophy, the University of Texas at Austin.
　　　　　ISBN 0-87462-141-0

#41 The Problem of Evil (1977) by Errol E. Harris, D.Litt., Distinguished Visiting Professor of Philosophy, Marquette University.
　　　　　ISBN 0-87462-142-9

#42 The Catholic University and the Faith (1978) by Francis C. Wade, S.J., professor of philosophy, Marquette University.

ISBN 0-87462-143-7

#43 St. Thomas and Historicity (1979) by Armand Maurer, C.S.B., professor of philosophy, University of Toronto and the Pontifical Institute of Mediaeval Studies, Toronto.

ISBN 0-87462-144-5

#44 Does God Have a Nature? (1980) by Alvin Plantinga, Ph.D., professor of philosophy, Calvin College, Grand Rapids, Michigan.

ISBN 0-87462-145-3

#45 Rhyme and Reason: St. Thomas and Modes of Discourse (1981) by Ralph McInerny, Ph.D., professor of Medieval Studies, University of Notre Dame.   ISBN 0-87462-148-8

#46 The Gift: Creation (1982) by Kenneth L. Schmitz, Ph.D., professor of philosophy at Trinity College, University of Toronto.

ISBN 0-87462-149-6

#47 How Philosophy Begins (1983) by Beatrice H. Zedler, Ph.D., Professor of Philosophy at Marquette University.

ISBN 0-87462-151-8

#48 The Reality of the Historical Past (1984) by Paul Ricoeur, professor of philosophy, University of Paris.

ISBN 0-87462-152-6

Uniform format, cover and binding.

Copies of this Aquinas Lecture and the others in the series are obtainable from:

Marquette University Press
Marquette University
Milwaukee, Wisconsin 53233, U.S.A.